Seth Is Six

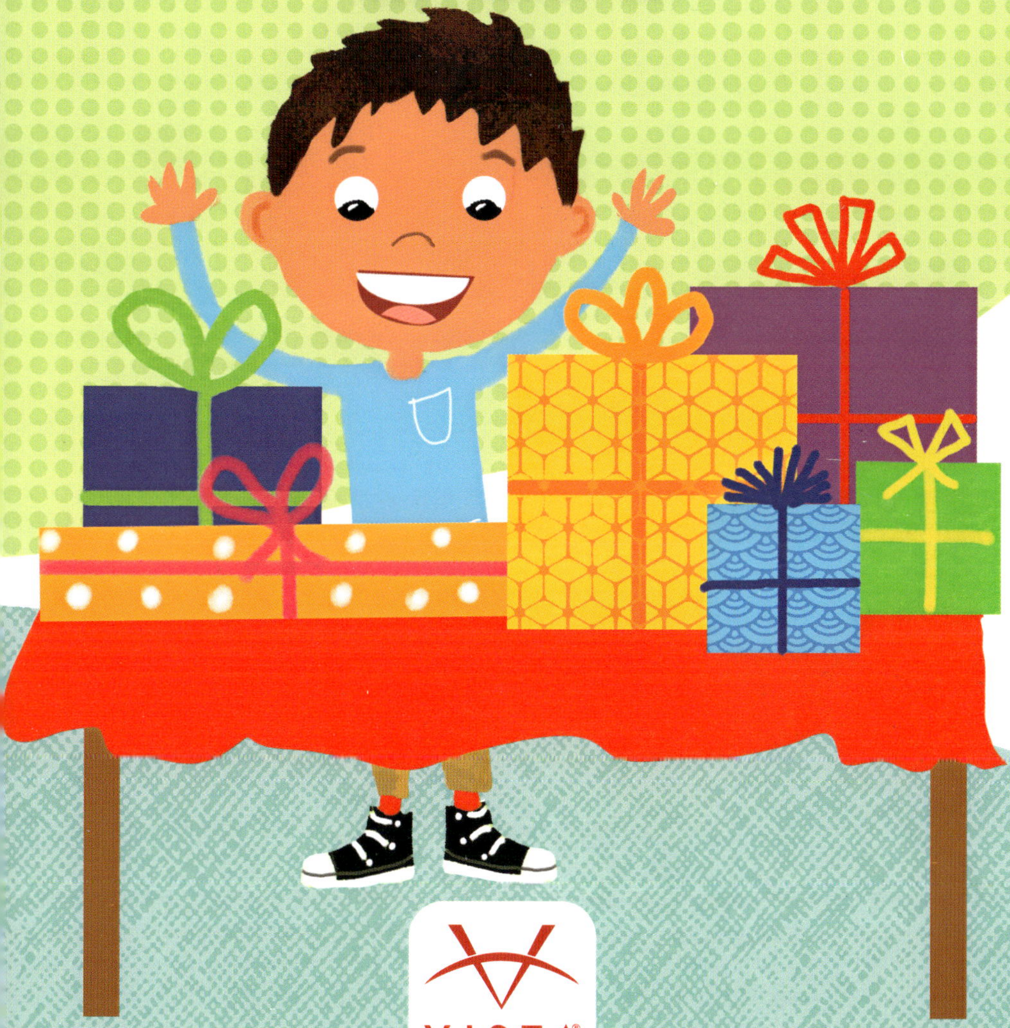

Boston, Massachusetts

This is Seth.

It is his big day!

Seth is six!

Seth got six boxes.

Each one looks different.

What is in each box?

One of the boxes has a bat in it.

Seth will have so much fun!

One of the boxes
has a red wig in it.

Put it on, Seth!

Two of the boxes have frogs in them.

Can Seth catch the frogs?

The last two boxes have foxes in them.

Did Seth wish for two foxes?

Seth is six.

Seth gets six boxes.

It is fun to be six!